Blessed Pier Giorgio Frassati

Blessed Pier Giorgio Frassati
Journey to the Summit

Written by
Ana Maria Vazquez
and
Jennings Dean

Illustrated by
Don Stewart

Pauline
BOOKS & MEDIA
Boston

Library of Congress Cataloging-in-Publication Data

Vazquez, Ana Maria.

Blessed Pier Giorgio Frassati : journey to the summit /
written by Ana Maria Vazquez and Jennings Dean ;
illustrated by Don Stewart.

    p. cm. — (Encounter the saints series ; 18)

  ISBN 0-8198-1165-3 (pbk.)

  1. Frassati, Pier Giorgio, 1901–1925. 2. Blessed—Italy—
Biography. I. Dean, Jennings. II. Stewart, Don, 1961–
III. Title. IV. Series.

  BX4705.F735V39 2004

  282'.092—dc22

                           2004004392

Published by Pauline Books & Media, 50 Saint Paul's
Avenue, Boston, MA 02130-3491. www.pauline.org.

Printed in the U.S.A.

VSAUSAPEOILL9-1J11-07763 1165-3

Pauline Books & Media is the publishing house of the
Daughters of St. Paul, an international congregation of
women religious serving the Church with the communica-
tions media.

4   5   6   7   8   9   15   14   13   12   11

Encounter the Saints Series

Blesseds Jacinta and Francisco Marto
Shepherds of Fatima

Blessed John Paul II
The People's Pope

Blessed Pier Giorgio Frassati
Journey to the Summit

Blessed Teresa of Calcutta
Missionary of Charity

Journeys with Mary
Apparitions of Our Lady

Saint Anthony of Padua
Fire and Light

Saint Bakhita of Sudan
Forever Free

Saint Bernadette Soubirous
And Our Lady of Lourdes

Saint Clare of Assisi
A Light for the World

Saint Damien of Molokai
Hero of Hawaii

Saint Edith Stein
Blessed by the Cross

Saint Elizabeth Ann Seton
Daughter of America

Saint Faustina Kowalska
Messenger of Mercy

Saint Frances Xavier Cabrini
Cecchina's Dream

Saint Francis of Assisi
Gentle Revolutionary

Saint Ignatius of Loyola
For the Greater Glory of God

Saint Isaac Jogues
With Burning Heart

Saint Joan of Arc
God's Soldier

Saint John Vianney
A Priest for All People

Saint Juan Diego
And Our Lady of Guadalupe

Saint Katharine Drexel
The Total Gift

Saint Martin de Porres
Humble Healer

Saint Maximilian Kolbe
Mary's Knight

Saint Paul
The Thirteenth Apostle

Saint Pio of Pietrelcina
Rich in Love

Saint Teresa of Avila
Joyful in the Lord

Saint Thérèse of Lisieux
The Way of Love

For other children's titles on the saints,
visit our Web site: www.pauline.org.

CONTENTS

1

AN EASTER GIFT

It was April 6, 1901, a brilliant spring morning and Holy Saturday as well. As the inhabitants of Turin, Italy made their last minute preparations for Easter, members and servants of the Frassati household happily bustled about welcoming the family's first baby.

"Che bello!" ("How beautiful!") admired the cook.

Adelaide Frassati, a well-known, talented painter looked lovingly at her new son. *He's my Easter gift,* she thought with a smile, *a living jewel.*

Alfredo Frassati, a man of considerable achievement and fame, director and owner of one of Italy's leading newspapers, *La Stampa*, gazed down at his baby, planning his future even then. *Here is my son and heir, the one who will take over the direction of* La Stampa, he mused. *Here is the future of my family and my name.*

Neither parent had the faintest idea of what their tiny baby would grow up to be. They named him Pier Giorgio: Pier (Peter) in honor of the apostle Saint Peter, to whom Jesus entrusted his holy Church, and Giorgio (George) after Saint George who slew the dragon.

A year after Pier Giorgio was born, there followed a baby girl, named Luciana.

At first, Pier Giorgio wasn't too sure about the new arrival. It seemed to him that she got most of the attention. Later, he called her Tatanina. (He called himself Dodo, because he couldn't pronounce Pier Giorgio.)

Luciana and Pier Giorgio were great friends, but they were lonely too. Instead of going to school, they were educated at home by tutors, as was the custom then in upper class families. "I wish we could play games with other children," Pier Giorgio would sometimes say with a sigh. "It would be nice," Luciana would answer, "but you know that Mama and Papa won't let us."

As happens with all brothers and sisters, Pier Giorgio and Luciana occasionally got into some good fights. "Dodo," their mother warned, "you must never hit your sister. You're older; you should know better. Besides, boys should never fight with girls."

Mr. Frassati was even stricter than his wife. Once he severely scolded Pier Giorgio for fighting with Luciana. "A man should not behave like this!" he exclaimed. "A son like this cannot be loved by his father." This last remark really hurt five-year-old Pier Giorgio, who loved everyone in his family. He wrote this note to his father:

Dear beautiful little Daddy,

I love you. Just so you will be happy, I will not hit Luciana anymore.

Happy Birthday. I will pray to the Infant Jesus for you.

A big kiss from your Dodo.

So Pier Giorgio learned to suffer in silence, letting Luciana get the best of him in their little battles. He even had scratches to prove it.... But the two still loved each other.

Although they were wealthy, Mr. and Mrs. Frassati spent very little money on gifts for their children. The stern parents considered presents to be unnecessary. But Pier Giorgio and Luciana were learning other kinds of lessons from their grandmother, their mother's mother, Mrs. Linda Ametis. Grandmother Ametis took them to Mass and taught them about Jesus. She was a true Christian and a devoted Catholic. It was she whom the children felt close to. It was she who made sure that the love of God filled their hearts.

Grandmother Ametis lived in a beautiful country house, called *Pollone*, about fifty miles from Turin. She loved flowers, and she taught Pier Giorgio about them. "See, Dodo, these are lilies. These are roses," she instructed. "You must be careful with the roses and cut them a special way."

Pier Giorgio grew to love the flowers in his grandmother's garden. Once he was holding a lovely cut rose when a nun came into the garden to visit. He rushed up to her saying, "Please, Sister, give this rose to Jesus. Be sure you tell him it's from me!"

Pier Giorgio loved to think about Jesus. One evening the Frassatis were hosting a very fancy party with many important people in attendance. Pier Giorgio was in bed when a disturbing thought occurred to him. He jumped up and raced downstairs in his pajamas. Maneuvering his way through evening dresses and tuxedos, he ran up to his mother. "Mama, Mama, was Jesus an orphan?" he panted.

The guests watched in amusement. But Mrs. Frassati was embarrassed and angered by her son's silly behavior...until she looked down into his tiny, tormented face. Her heart melted. "No, Pier Giorgio," she said gently. "Jesus was not an orphan. He had

God our Father in heaven as his father and the Blessed Mother as his mother. Not only that, but he had Saint Joseph, the carpenter, as his father on earth."

"That's good!" the little boy sighed in relief.

2

LESSONS IN LOVE

"Tatanina, you're putting jam over your butter!" Pier Giorgio warned at breakfast one morning.

Luciana, whose chin was sticky with jam, mumbled, "I love jam and butter."

"But you know Papa doesn't permit that," Pier Giorgio shot back. "You must have one or the other. They are very expensive!"

Being careful about money was an iron rule in the well-to-do Frassati household.

The family dined in a large corner room of the first floor of their duplex. Two dark oaken sideboards heavy with carvings stood against the wall. The family sat at a big old-fashioned table with matching wooden chairs. That evening a scene erupted when a frowning Mr. Frassati asked his wife, "Adelaide, what did you do with all the money I gave you last week? I'd like to know what you spent it on."

Mrs. Frassati jumped up from the table, spilling wine on her dress, and rushed from the room in tears. The children watched in silence. Pier Giorgio put down his fork. He wasn't hungry anymore. Such episodes happened often. They made a deep impression on Pier Giorgio.

There was, however, another stronger side to his mother. She loved the outdoors and took the children on beautiful mountain walks. Turin, Italy is in the Piedmont region (Piedmont means "foot of the mountains") of the majestic snow clad Alps. You could go skiing, sledding, and climbing in these mountains. Pier Giorgio loved these outings. He eventually became an excellent climber and an accomplished skier.

Mr. Frassati also loved to play all kinds of games with his children. He would come home from his office and get things going. "Let's go out to the garden," he'd say. "Pier Giorgio, show us some somersaults. Luciana, bring over the ball."

Pier Giorgio's legs were growing strong and sturdy, but his heart was growing, too, in love and understanding of others. He felt a special compassion for those who were suffering in any way—the sad, the sick, the poor, and the elderly. One day, when he was about six, he opened the door to a poorly dressed woman, clutching a child by the hand. "Little boy," she pleaded, "can you help us? We need money. We have no food."

"Wait! I can give you something!"

"My parents aren't home," Pier Giorgio sadly explained. "I don't have any..."

Suddenly noticing that the child was barefoot, he continued with a smile. "Wait! I *can* give you something!" Pier Giorgio reached down, took off his shoes, and happily handed them to the young boy.

Another time, he visited an orphanage with his grandfather, who had built the orphans a school. While Pier Giorgio was having lunch there, he saw one boy sitting all alone at the end of a table.

"He has something ugly on his face," a youngster next to Pier Giorgio pointed out. "Nobody *ever* sits near him."

It was true. The poor boy had a terrible skin infection which kept the other children away from him. Pier Giorgio immediately took his plate and spoon and went and sat down beside the lonely little boy, sharing his bowl of soup with him. He did this very quietly—almost no one noticed.

Pier Giorgio learned to read and write when he was only five, but he did have a problem with reading. "I can't stand this stuff!" he used to complain in frustration. "I want to go out and play."

In 1913 twelve-year-old Pier Giorgio and eleven-year-old Luciana entered a public school, Massimo D'Azeglio. Luciana had an easy time of it, but Pier Giorgio did not.

"Luciana, I'll never get all this home-work done," he would moan. "I don't understand this Latin...."

His worst nightmare came true when report cards came out.

He had failed Latin.

3

FACING THE MUSIC

Called into his father's presence to explain his grades, Pier Giorgio's heart sank into his shoes.

Mr. Frassati was seated at his desk, his face more sad than angry. "Pier Giorgio," he began, "we have to do something about these grades of yours."

Pier Giorgio wished he were up in the beautiful snowy Alps instead of here in this stifling office. "I know, Papa," he mumbled. "I'm sorry."

His father was still talking, but Pier Giorgio's thoughts were suddenly far away, revisiting a better time, a happier place. It was an early fall morning when he was eight years old. Pier Giorgio's parents had announced that they were taking him on a mountain climb up to *Lago Nero* (Black Lake). It was to be his first mountain hike with grownups.

He had awakened when it was still dark. His mother, his father, and his aunt had bundled him into the car. Off they had gone to the place from which they would start their climb. There they had met the porter who would accompany them and carry their supplies. Pier Giorgio had been too excited to be sleepy. His happiness would have been complete if Luciana had also come along. But she had stayed home and slept.

Pier Giorgio saw himself eagerly climbing the mountain again. He heard his father call out for all to hear, "You're a strong fellow, Georgie. I'm proud of you!"

There was so much beauty to see. The clear blue sky. Immense rocky ravines. Majestic mountain peaks blanketed in white. Pier Giorgio felt so very close to God. From that day on, the mountains would always be for him a refuge, a special place to be alone with God.

His thoughts now jumped to the wonderful summers he had spent at the beach by the Mediterranean Sea. He remembered the first time he had looked out at the sea. It seemed to never end. Pier Giorgio had never been afraid of anything before, but this water scared him. It was alive. It was moving. Maybe it would swallow him!

"Pier Giorgio, let's see you swim!" his mother had teasingly called.

He had started to protest, but it was too late. She had thrown him in. His life preserver had kept him bobbing in the waves. And soon enough he was swimming. Later in life, Pier Giorgio would actually become a champion swimmer.

A final happy scene came rushing into his mind. His father was introducing him to his famous horse, Parsifal. Irish thoroughbreds were famous for being high strung and hard to handle, but Pier Giorgio loved this beautiful horse, and would ride him for hours on end. One day he would become a very gifted horseman....

"Pier Giorgio!" he heard from very far away. "Are you listening to me?"

Startled, Pier Giorgio looked up at his father's stern expression.

"Yes, Papa. I'm listening," he sheepishly lied.

"Your mother is very upset by all this, and she has come to a decision, as have I," Mr. Frassati was saying. "You shall go to school with the Jesuits. If you can't learn there, you can't learn anywhere."

Pier Giorgio felt as if he'd just been sentenced to prison. How would he *ever* stay indoors and study all day?

4

A HAPPY SURPRISE

That summer Pier Giorgio would go to the mountains with his mother alone. She had, more or less, forgiven him for the Latin episode. But she had also sternly reminded him, "You must excel. Never waste time. Never daydream. Always be on time. Always be strong!"

On this very sunny day, Adelaide Frassati marched up the steep path above *Pollone* to a site where she had chosen to paint. Pier Giorgio carried her paint box and brushes. She carried the easel.

"You're a good son," she said with a smile.

Pier Giorgio's heart warmed. His mother was so beautiful—just as his father always said.

"Can we go higher, Mama?" he asked.

"No, this will do. I can see what I have to from here," she replied.

Pier Giorgio could have climbed higher, carrying the easel and all. He was sturdy and athletic. Mrs. Frassati gave him an approving glance. *I've made him this way,* she thought. She wanted her children to be strong and healthy, and, above all, true to themselves and successful. She remembered how Pier Giorgio had mastered a steep Alpine climb they had made together to ten thousand feet. She had wanted him to be able to face fatigue and hunger. And he had passed with flying colors.

"What are you going to paint?" Pier Giorgio asked, opening the box with the brushes.

"There's a lovely view of the flower beds from here," Mrs. Frassati answered. "I shall paint beautiful colors."

Pier Giorgio set up the easel while his mother adjusted her palette. He set a partially completed canvas on the easel. It had all his favorite flowers on it.

"I'm very pleased with you, Pier Giorgio," Mrs. Frassati admitted. "You have great strength, and you don't give up easily."

"Thank you, Mama," he smiled.

Pier Giorgio watched his mother make magic on her canvas. Shapes became hills and gardens. Colors jumped out at him. *It's a special gift to be able to create beauty like that,* he thought. Later in the day, Mrs. Frassati sat watching her son. "Our hopes are in you, Georgie," she confided. "You'll take your father's place as the man of our family."

Pier Giorgio nodded.

"We can't depend on your sister because she's a girl." Mrs. Frassati touched her brush to the paint. "Yes, Luciana is only a girl. You will be the one to take over *La Stampa*. You are the hope of the Frassati-Ametis family."

"Mama," Pier Giorgio uneasily broke in, "you know I have a hard time in school. Everything is easy for Luciana."

His mother stabbed the palette with her brush. Her gray eyes fixed Pier Giorgio in one of her famous penetrating stares. "It makes no difference; she is a girl. You are the man."

Mrs. Frassati's attitude reflected the opinions and customs of her day. The early twentieth century was a time when men were considered more important than women in most societies. No matter what Luciana did, she would always be second to Pier Giorgio in her parents' eyes.

Pier Giorgio wished he were better in school. His parents were counting on him to do important things. He didn't know if he was up to it. He would ask Jesus to help him.

❖ ❖ ❖

That same year something wonderful happened. A telegram arrived one morning.

Aunt Elena opened it, and a smile spread across her kind face. She showed the telegram to Pier Giorgio. He could hardly believe what he read! He ran to find Luciana, and the two of them raced to the dining room and slipped the message under their mother's plate.

When the family sat down to supper that evening, Mr. Frassati eagerly plunged into his favorite *gnocchi* smothered in creamy cheese sauce. He paused when he saw the expectant faces turned toward his wife. Pier Giorgio gave his mother's plate a tiny push. The edge of the telegram peeked out.

His mother moved the plate and picked up the message. Her hand began to tremble as she read it. Tears of joy filled her eyes.

Pier Giorgio gave her a big kiss. Luciana hugged her. Mr. Frassati raised his glass and toasted his wife.

Victor Emmanuel, the king of Italy, had just purchased one of Mrs. Frassati's paintings being shown at the *Venice Biennale,* one of Italy's most prestigious art shows!

Pier Giorgio watched his mother. He knew how hard she had worked for perfection in her art. He was so proud of her.

That evening Mrs. Frassati didn't run from the table.

5

GROWING PAINS

Soon it was Mr. Frassati's turn to receive a great honor. Some months after the king bought Mrs. Frassati's painting, Mr. Frassati was appointed senator. Again the family rejoiced.

That same year, 1913, Pier Giorgio entered a Jesuit school, the *Istituto Sociale*, and, for the first time, was separated from Luciana. Now he was on his own with other boys.

"How is it going with those strict Jesuits?" Luciana asked after the first week.

"The Latin teacher has been great," Pier Giorgio replied with a big smile. "He doesn't seem to mind going over it until I get it. I was really having a hard time, but I'm doing a lot better now."

"Don't give up, Georgie," Luciana encouraged. "I know you can do it."

But Pier Giorgio had something more important than Latin on his mind, and that was the Holy Eucharist. He had noticed on Sundays that his mother and his Aunt Elena, just as many others at that time, rarely received Holy Communion. In those days going to Communion on Christmas and Easter was thought to be enough.

But it was not enough for Pier Giorgio. He wanted to feel closer to Jesus and receive Communion every day. Pier Giorgio had watched the priests, monks, and nuns receive the Holy Eucharist every day with a small, select group of lay people. He wanted to be a part of this.

Father Pietro Lombardi was one of his friends and mentors at school. One day, Pier Giorgio asked him, "Father, could I go to daily Communion too?"

"I don't see why not," Father Lombardi responded, "but I think you should first ask for your mother's permission."

When Pier Giorgio approached his mother with the idea, she put up some major resistance. "So you're going to run off to Mass every day with all the old ladies!" she exclaimed. "You're going to become a narrow minded Catholic. No other children do this. I don't know what's wrong with you, Pier Giorgio. I absolutely forbid it!"

"Mama, I—"

"It's out of the question."

"Please, Mama..."

The subject was closed, temporarily.

For the next few days, Pier Giorgio kept after his mother about the needed permission.

"Why are you always so stubborn? You are a real *Piemontese*—with a head of stone."

"But, Mama, please..."

"One thing I'll say for you, you never give up."

Pier Giorgio's eyes filled with hope.

"All right, all right. I give you my permission," Mrs. Frassati finally relented.

Pier Giorgio was overjoyed. At Mass in the morning, he would pray for his family and friends, especially for his mother and father. "Dearest Jesus, help my mother and father understand each other. Please don't let my mother think I'm weak because I love you."

The parish priest once confided to Pier Giorgio's grandmother, Mrs. Ametis, "Pier Giorgio is a very unusual boy. When he receives Communion, his face is transformed."

Pier Giorgio was firm in his beliefs and stood up for his ideals even when they were unpopular. Once another student came up to him in the school courtyard. "Hey, Georgie," he taunted, "you're a real slave of the priests, always serving at Mass. The clergy are a bunch of no-goods. My dad says so." Anti-clericalism, being critical of the clergy, was very common in Italy at that time. It was a serious problem for faithful Catholics and the Church.

Pier Giorgio slowly turned around. Other boys were listening. He really didn't want to start anything, but he couldn't let this go by. It was true—and sad—that there were lazy and immoral priests. But that was no reason to condemn the dedicated ones. "You have no idea what you're talking about," he firmly told the offender. "I hope you'll take back what you just said."

When the boy started cursing instead, Pier Giorgio took a swing at him. At first the troublemaker was too surprised to respond. But then the fight got going, and Pier Giorgio followed up by knocking him down. At that point, the boy's followers turned on Pier Giorgio and threw him in the dirt. Pier Giorgio's friends rallied to help him, and the result was a first class battle. The priest responsible for student discipline broke it up and gave everyone demerits.

Later, eyeing Pier Giorgio's bandages and bruises, his father sternly remarked, "It looks like you've been to war."

"What do you mean by this? It's the way of savages!" his mother scolded.

"I was standing up for what I believe in, Mama," replied Pier Giorgio.

Mr. Frassati broke into a smile. "Well, then, Georgie, I hope you gave as good as you got. I think you did. It's always necessary for a man to stand up for his ideals."

Mrs. Frassati frowned and turned away.

Luciana looked admiringly at her brother. She always took her father's side.

6

A Difference of Opinion

The year 1914 saw Europe plunged into a terrible and cruel war—known as World War I. Poisoned gas made its first appearance during this conflict. Huge gaseous clouds struck down hundreds of soldiers. Writhing in agony, their lungs seared and burning, they fell to the muddy earth of the battle fields. Some lived; but many died. Others were maimed for life.

The tank, which bore down mercilessly on soldiers and civilians alike, also came into use for the first time at the end of this catastrophe. One battle in France saw as many as 350,000 soldiers wounded or killed in a single day of fighting. It was a hell on earth, and not only on land, for airplanes brought the fighting to the skies.

When the war started in August of 1914, no one had any idea of the horrors it would bring. Austria-Hungary, with her ally, Germany, were known as the Central Powers. These countries marched off to battle Russia. Russia was helped by Britain and France. These latter three countries were known as the Allies.

In September of that year, Alfredo Frassati, sitting at his desk at *La Stampa*, remarked to one of his colleagues, "This war is a catastrophe. Italy must have no part of it."

Mr. Banzatti nodded his agreement. "It would certainly not be in our best interest. War would ruin us."

Mr. Frassati rested his elbows on his desk. "You know as well as I do that there are those who would go to war in the wink of an eye to get back the Trentino and the Alto Adige—land that was originally ours."

"I know, I know," retorted Mr. Banzatti, rubbing his forehead as if the very thought gave him a headache. "They would sacrifice the lives of our young men for a piece of earth."

"But it's tough to argue with them, Banzatti. The Austrians stole that land from us many years ago. It *really* is Italy's. Still, how do we convince these warriors that this is *not* a good time to attempt to get it back?"

"I have no idea," Mr. Banzatti said wearily, "but we'll fight them all the way with our newspaper. And we have our friends."

Yes, Mr. Frassati thought sadly, *we have many good and powerful friends, but some of them, like General Cadorna, are determined that Italy should enter this senseless war.*

Pier Giorgio shared his father's beliefs and was also a neutralist, someone who wanted to stay on the sidelines and not enter the war.

At school one day, a student named Mario Attilo attacked Mr. Banzatti's son, Camillo, and Pier Giorgio, yelling, "You're both traitors—just like your fathers!" He called them cowards and worse.

Camillo grabbed Mario by his lapels and boxed his ears. Pier Giorgio kept out of the fight this time. He had his reasons.

When Pier Giorgio showed up for supper that night, he found that the story of Camillo's heroics was the subject of conversation. He, himself, had disappointed his family.

"You're never on time for meals," his mother lashed out at him. "You're constantly distracted. And by what? Going on like an old lady. Why didn't you help Camillo out? You're good for nothing...."

His father followed up with, "Georgie, this was a golden opportunity to defend our position on the war, our paper, our family, our cause. And what did you do? You stood around and watched.... I'm ashamed of you."

"Papa," said Pier Giorgio quietly, "it was two against one. It wouldn't have been fair. Tomorrow it will be my turn to defend us and the neutralist cause."

7

CHALLENGES

Pier Giorgio felt a lump in his throat. He wished his family would understand what he had to do. He got up an hour earlier in the morning so he could go to Mass. No one else in the family did that. Why did *he* have to? A certain sadness began to weigh him down. He no longer shared secrets with Luciana. He had greatly disappointed his mother and father. They openly told him so.

In order to preserve peace at home, Pier Giorgio became more and more withdrawn. He wasn't angry at his parents and sister. He just didn't have much to say to them anymore.

For some time now he had been saving his streetcar ticket money to give to the poor. Because of this, he had to run home from school and was often late for meals. His mother would complain, "Where were you, Pier Giorgio? What were you doing? Why are you always late?"

He couldn't get a part-time job to earn money because of his family's distinguished position in Italian society. He was a

Frassati, and he was to be educated to take over *La Stampa*. Young boys of his social class did not work in those days. They went to school and did long, arduous hours of homework. They were very well educated in many subjects and were driven by their teachers to excel.

Pier Giorgio found an outlet for his pent-up feelings and energy in his passion for soccer. He played forward and loved it. One day a friend commented, "You know, Giorgio, you're the best man on the team. You could go and play in the big league some day. You really have what it takes."

Pier Giorgio dreamed of joining the national team, the *Juve* of Turin. But this could never happen because of his place in society and the expectations of his parents. He could never become a professional athlete; it just wouldn't be proper. His future at *La Stampa* was the only thing that mattered—to everyone but him.

But Pier Giorgio was making many friends, and they brightened his life. He loved to go skiing with them. They would go plummeting down the great Alps near Turin. Pier Giorgio was fearless. "No one can downhill like Georgie!" admiring friends exclaimed. "He flies like the wind."

"Georgie, you're the best man on the team!"

He also hiked often in his beloved mountains. In their vast whiteness, he felt closer to God, mysteriously happier and more alive. For all of his life the mountains would remain his great source of inspiration. He could see in them a reflection of the all-powerful Creator of the universe.

If only he could feel the same way about school.... If only he could be like Luciana, who seemed to get through every class without any effort. But Pier Giorgio was never at home in the classroom. Everyone knew that the "senator's son" was no scholar. It didn't matter. Pier Giorgio found happiness in his relationship with God, in nature, in sports, and in his friends.

He was always a good and sympathetic listener. One friend would say to another, "If you have a problem, go to Pier Giorgio. He'll help you." Once Pier Giorgio asked a couple of his friends to pray the rosary with him. They did. This was the beginning of something new. From then on he quietly influenced many young people to come closer to God.

8

THE MAKING OF A SAINT

Pier Giorgio waved at his friends as they surged out the doors of the *Istituto Sociale*. School was out for the day.

"Hey, Giorgio, see you at soccer!" called a classmate.

"Be sure you show up," added another.

Glancing back, Pier Giorgio noticed one of his friends walking dejectedly, his eyes fixed on the ground.

Pier Giorgio quickly retraced his steps. "What's wrong, Paolo?" he asked. "Why all the gloom?"

The boy shook his head. "Georgie," he moaned. "I'm in so much trouble at home—and here, too. I'm in a real mess."

Pier Giorgio nodded sympathetically. "What's wrong at home?"

"You know that I'm not exactly a whiz at math," Paolo said with a sigh. "In fact, I'm not any good at any of my subjects. The problem is that my dad wants me to go into his business, Georgie." He turned and looked back at the building. "My grades are terrible. My parents are going to cut off my soccer if I don't start doing better soon."

"I know just what you mean, Paolo," Pier Giorgio said understandingly. "I'm not good in school either. My mom is always talking about how I should get better grades. She's very strict."

"But the Latin teacher says we should all imitate you," Paolo replied.

"He also said I wasn't much of a scholar," Pier Giorgio chuckled.

"But you work hard at it," Paolo insisted, "probably harder than anyone in the class."

"Still, my grades aren't that great," Pier Giorgio admitted, shaking his head.

"I think my parents hate me," Paolo suddenly burst out.

"No, Paolo," Pier Giorgio said thoughtfully, "they don't hate you. They're just strict, like mine. Listen, I have an idea."

"What?"

"Let's say a prayer for help with your problems at home."

Paolo looked totally shocked. "Come on, Georgie. You've got to be kidding..."

"I'm not," Pier Giorgio smiled. "What have you got to lose?"

"I pray at Mass and at meals. It's boring."

"Will you come and pray with me?" Pier Giorgio asked.

Paolo shrugged his shoulders and reluctantly followed his friend into a nearby church.

They genuflected, then knelt in the semi-darkness. Pier Giorgio made the sign of the cross and fixed his eyes on the tabernacle. Paolo looked distractedly around. After a few minutes he, too, slowly began to pray. Something was happening. Paolo could feel it. A kind of strength was coming from Pier Giorgio.

Back out in the sunlight, Pier Giorgio turned to his friend "Did you ask Jesus to help you?"

"Yes."

"How do you feel now?"

"A lot better," Paolo admitted. "I can't explain it, but I feel happy. Thanks, Georgie. Thanks a lot! See you at soccer practice!"

A priest who knew Pier Giorgio would say later that the real miracle of this extraordinary young man was his ability to attract others by his simple virtues and his sincere charity.

Later that evening at the Frassati apartment, Sister Angelica, Grandmother Ametis's nurse, came out into the hall to fetch a towel from the linen cupboard. The door to Pier Giorgio's room was slightly ajar, and she noticed a faint light. She looked in and was about to call to him when something stopped her. Pier Giorgio was kneeling by his bed praying, his face glowing with light. The nun stood rooted to the spot. *He's having a vision,* she said to herself, *a heavenly vision.* The realization troubled her. *Should I tell someone? My confessor? The pastor? No,* she decided, *I won't say a thing. This is Pier Giorgio's private time with God. And I'm an intruder.* Sister Angelica kept her secret for many years. She revealed what she saw that night only after Pier Giorgio's death.

9

YEARS OF TURMOIL

"We're at war! We're at war!" Pier Giorgio was shocked by the cries that filled the streets. Italy had joined Britain and France in the battle against Germany and Austria-Hungary. Senator Frassati's face showed his despair. It saddened him that his long time friend, General Cadorna, was celebrating his nation's entry into the bloody conflict.

At first, everyone was patriotic. Flags waved. Soldiers marched in uniforms to the strains of martial band music. The honor of the nation would be saved. The *Trentino* and the *Alto Adige* stolen from Italy by the Austrians would be taken back. Italy's soldiers would win renown on the battle-field. The nation was ready for war.

The year was 1915, the same year in which Pier Giorgio made his Confirmation. After the ceremony, Pier Giorgio was having his picture taken with his family. "Georgie, stop laughing," his mother admonished, "this is a serious occasion." Pier Giorgio saw nothing wrong with wanting to share his great joy with his family and friends.

That year found the fourteen-year-old becoming more and more involved with the poor. He would go to help his "special cases," bringing food and medicine he bought with his own money to shut-ins. Everyone in the slums knew him. A fellow student once asked, "Georgie, how can you stand the smell of those filthy apartment houses? I don't understand why you go there..."

Pier Giorgio answered slowly, "The poor people I try to help are often very close to Jesus. Remember how he told us, 'The good you do for the poor, you also do for me.'"

Pier Giorgio joined the war effort by studying agriculture at the *Istituto Bonafous*. He obtained a diploma in agronomy, the science of crop production. His course covered the whole process of harvesting wheat and storing it in barns, and he applied this practical knowledge to directing the farm work at *Pollone*. The fact that he could ride a horse was also a great asset in the fields. At night, he would return home with some farm produce for his family ...unless he met someone needy along the way.

Pier Giorgio enjoyed making the 53-mile bike ride from Turin to *Pollone* with his friend Carlo Bellingeri. One day after the boys had stopped to visit Carlo's family, Pier Giorgio found himself staring dismally at the chain lock that had been torn from the banister of the house. His bike had been stolen, after all the effort he had made to save the money to buy it! Pier Giorgio shrugged his shoulders and managed a smile. "Maybe someone needs that bike more than I do," was all he said.

World War I continued. Friends and family lost their loved ones in the horrifying battles. Old-time friendships were swept away in the fury of wartime politics and opinions. The Frassati house became estranged from famous and respected friends who favored the war.

Pier Giorgio did his part, assisting the farmers to harvest the wheat and corn. He also helped Carolina Gola. Her husband, Giuseppe, the gardener at *Pollone*, had gone to war. Pier Giorgio still remembered his first meeting with the tall, sunburned farmer who had arrived years ago to take over the grounds of the family estate. He remembered the happy childhood days at Mrs. Gola's hearth. She would stir the *polenta* (mashed corn meal) while he and Luciana tossed chestnuts into the fire—an enjoyable activity not allowed in the strict atmosphere of their own home. When Mr. Gola returned from the war, he was amazed at the work Pier Giorgio had done. He was especially impressed with Pier Giorgio's success in growing potatoes, a very important staple during wartime food shortages.

Despite all Pier Giorgio's hard work, his father was always finding fault with him. Passing by Pier Giorgio's room one night, Mr. Frassati saw him kneeling in prayer. So much time "wasted," and for what? This devotion to a God whom the older Frassati barely believed in was just too much. Mr. Frassati immediately stormed to the rectory. "What have you done to my son?" he demanded of Monsignor Roccati, who had baptized Pier Giorgio as an infant. The monsignor, in full dignity, calmly faced Mr. Frassati's anger. "Perhaps, Senator, you would prefer him to fall asleep reading a dirty book?"

"Of course not..." came the embarrassed reply.

Pier Giorgio continued his hard work, especially among the poor. And his father remained perplexed at his son's behavior. "Georgie, where do you go most of the time? Why are you always late? Why do you always seem so distracted?" Alfredo

Frassati would shake his head in frustration. He had no idea of his son's activities on behalf of the poor and oppressed. This was especially ironic, since Mr. Frassati was always conscientious about society's obligations to the less fortunate.

The war dragged on. Soldiers trickled home from battle. One rainy afternoon, as Pier Giorgio walked down a Turin street, he saw a limping soldier struggling along in his ragged uniform. Pier Giorgio took the man's knapsack and carried it. He brought him to a shelter and got him food. From then on, the young man became a familiar visitor at the hospitals, bringing necessities, food, and even cigarettes to the wounded veterans. Pier Giorgio was everywhere. "How does he do it all?" a friend asked.

"I don't know," another admitted. "He's always out helping someone. I don't think he ever sleeps."

10

A New Road

"Viva Wilson! Viva Wilson!"

Pier Giorgio ran down to the piazza to join the excited crowd, adding his booming voice to those who greeted the American President, Woodrow Wilson, on his visit to Turin that day in 1919.

President Wilson's ideas for an international government especially touched the hearts of the idealistic young, filling them with optimism after the terrible years of World War I. They hoped that the League of Nations (later to become the United Nations) which Wilson had founded, would change the way of the world, prevent future wars, and keep countries from committing injustices against each other. Thousands of youthful faces greeted President Wilson as his motorcade made its way through the city. At the end of the day, Pier Giorgio found himself hoarse but happy. He and his friends had made their feelings known. They yearned for a beautiful new world—a world at peace.

In the previous year Pier Giorgio had pursued his mining engineering studies at the Polytechnic in Turin. He had also managed to keep his diligent work for the poor hidden from the notice of his busy parents. In the little spare time he had, he enjoyed his favorite sports: mountain climbing and skiing.

"Hey, Giorgio," his friends would call out to him, "see you at the bottom!"

Pier Giorgio would plunge down the slopes with incredible speed. He loved it all: the wide open spaces, the rush of wind against his face, the skis racing beneath him, the glint of the sun on the powdered snow. The mountains nourished his spirit.

He continued to go to Mass every day that he could, and he never missed praying his daily rosary. He still kept his habit of saying his evening prayers kneeling by his bedside, as Sister Angelica had seen him do as a child. Pier Giorgio never allowed the breakneck speed of his ordinary, everyday life to interfere with his spiritual life. He put first things first: Mass and prayer.

Pier Giorgio had seen with his own eyes, and up close, the poverty and despair of the less fortunate, the forgotten citizens of the world. Just before beginning his university studies, he had joined the Society of Saint Vincent de Paul. Membership in this group gave him even more opportunities for serving the poor. Pier Giorgio, unlike most of the politicians and charitable do-gooders of his day, became intimately involved with the pain and suffering of his brothers and sisters. He saw the poor as God's children and considered them part of his own family.

Working for the Saint Vincent Society, he visited the city slums, bringing encouragement and cheer, not to mention food and medicine. He regarded the welfare of the poor as his personal responsibility, never something that someone else should take care of. He not only truly believed Saint Paul's teaching that charity is the greatest of all virtues, but he acted upon it in an astonishing way. He was like no other person, priest or layman, that the poor had ever seen. He loved them...and they knew it.

As if he weren't busy enough, Pier Giorgio also joined the Federation of Italian Catholic Students, known as FUCI. At their local FUCI center he and his friends held discussions about anything and everything: politics, religion, world events. They also played games of all types. Pier Giorgio was one of the best at pool. What he *wasn't* good at was singing. When a song got started on group picnics, hikes or bicycle rides, it wasn't long before someone would good-naturedly shout, "Giorgio, you're off key!"

"It doesn't matter," he'd yell back, "as long as I keep singing!"

Political involvement, his spiritual growth, and his social activities had opened Pier Giorgio's eyes to the world in a fresh way. He became more conscious of what was going on around him. He saw that charity was needed not only from private sources. He felt that the city itself should enact laws and provide funds to care for the poor and homeless. He began to branch out, to look for new ways to help the poor. His beliefs were becoming more and more concrete—something he would defend to the death.

One time, Pier Giorgio and his friend Curio Chiaraviglio went to the Fiat Automobile factory to try to prevent the underpaid, disgruntled workers from rioting. Upon arriving at the plant, the two young men faced the Communists and the very anti-Catholic workers who dominated the factory.

Standing beside Pier Giorgio, Curio met the angry stares of the mob. He took a few steps back. "Georgie," he whispered urgently, "this is no time to be wearing your Catholic Youth badge. Take it off! You know how they hate the Church. They'll beat us up for sure...."

Pier Giorgio quietly stood his ground. "I won't take it off," he responded. "It's part of who I am. I wear it because I believe in my Faith and in my Church."

A tense silence followed. Something about Pier Giorgio had registered with these rough men and commanded their respect. The Communists allowed Pier Giorgio and his Catholicism among them, and the workers' riot was avoided.

Curio felt a surge of relief as they left the Fiat factory. Pier Giorgio slapped him on the shoulder. "Life must be lived well," he exclaimed with a smile, "following true and sound principles. It's never enough to simply get along. No, that's not for us, Curio. That's not for us."

11

FRIEND TO ALL

One morning, Teresa, a maid in the palace of the Contessa Giuseppina Pesce dei Rechelmy, opened the door to a very handsome, smiling young man.

She ushered the visitor into the entrance hall with its embroidered antique wall hangings and oil paintings. Smile or no, she would escort him no further.

"I would like to speak with the Contessa," explained the young man, ever so politely.

"Do you have an appointment, Signore?" The countess required all visitors to have appointments.

"No, I actually don't," the visitor admitted, "but we have much to discuss."

"But, Signore, she's always so busy...." Teresa nervously wrung her hands, unsure of what to do next. "You should really have made an appointment..."

"I promise I'll take all the blame if she's angry," the guest ventured.

He looked so honest and kind. Teresa decided to admit him—as far as the door to the library.

She went into the library alone. Sitting at a gilt edge writing desk, the countess was frowning over a sheaf of papers.

"A young man to see you, Signora Contessa," Teresa announced.

"Who is he?" the countess asked, without looking up.

The servant put her hand to her mouth. "Oh, Signora Contessa, I forgot to ask his name! I'm so sorry."

"Then he must be very handsome," replied Contessa Pesce, laying aside her papers.

"He is very respectably dressed, Signora," Teresa admitted.

"You should have gotten his name," the older woman admonished in a tired voice, "but, very well, bring him in."

The countess's dark eyes lit in recognition and her face broke into a welcoming smile when Pier Giorgio stepped into the room. "Pier Giorgio!" she greeted him. "How delightful!"

"I've come to thank you, Contessa, for all that you do for the Society of Saint Vincent de Paul," Pier Giorgio said, extending his hand. "Your generosity has made it possible for us to buy new dishes for the kitchen."

"Well, then how can we thank *you* for all that you do for the Society?" Contessa Pesce responded. "The many hours you spend working for the poor and neglected...you really are an extraordinary young man, Pier Giorgio. Please, sit down." The two went on to talk over plans for new charitable projects, including the opening of a day care center for the children of working mothers.

Pier Giorgio's goodness and enthusiasm coupled with his gratitude for any donations made to the poor inspired more and more wealthy benefactors to donate to his causes. Years later, Contessa Pesce still remembered the powerful impression the young man had made on her. She went so far as to say, "In Pier Giorgio Frassati there is the stuff that saints are made of."

It always amazed Carlo Florio how Pier Giorgio, his friend, managed to balance endless hours serving his poor while still keeping up with his difficult engineering studies. One particular incident stuck in Carlo's memory. It was the day Pier Giorgio said he needed help to carry groceries to a family in the slums. Carlo didn't want to go, but Pier Giorgio was counting on him. After all, they were friends....

Standing in front of the rundown building, Carlo thought, *Poor people are depressing. Why should I have to climb five stories to visit a stinking tenement?*

"I really don't want to do this, Georgie," he said aloud.

Pier Giorgio grabbed his arm. "My friends are desperately waiting for this food, Carlo. I've also brought medicine for the grandmother who's very sick. Please," he pleaded, "don't let me down. I really need you."

"Okay, Okay." Carlo grudgingly picked up an armload of groceries and followed Pier Giorgio up the creaking stairs. *Georgie has really gone overboard with all this,* he thought. *These are just poor people. They're certainly not my friends...*

The stairwell was full of bad smells. On the different landings, Carlo saw several miserable looking women with even more miserable looking children, pitifully thin and dressed in rags. "...Got to get out of here before I catch some terrible disease," Carlo mumbled beneath his breath. He suddenly noticed with horror that the floor board was missing from the step nearest the approaching landing. He could see all the way down to the ground floor. "Georgie, you're going to get us killed!" he yelled.

"Come on," Pier Giorgio calmly urged. "We're only at the fourth floor. We have one more to go. Just hold on to those groceries. You'll be fine."

He cares more for the food than he does for me, thought Carlo.

Arriving at the fifth floor, Pier Giorgio knocked on a door at the head of the stairs. "San Carlo, protect us," muttered Carlo as the door creaked open and a tiny blotched face peeked out. Carlo thought he would faint. A monstrous odor overwhelmed him. Nausea rose in his throat. "Georgie, what have you gotten us into?" he protested.

Paying no attention, Pier Giorgio stepped into the apartment. Carlo had no choice but to follow. Eyeing the little boy who had answered the door, Carlo was struck by his bowlegs and strangely shaped head. Carlo suspected he had rickets, a disease that deforms the bones of children who don't get proper nutrition.

The one-room apartment was in darkness except for a shadow of light coming from a lone dirty window. The family had no heat. The room held a tiny stove, but the coal and wood supply had long since run out. Cracked pottery sat atop a splintered old oak sideboard. Carlo could see no evidence of food anywhere. In the gloom, he could barely make out mismatched chairs and broken floor tiles.

A tattered sheet curtained off an area. When the little boy pulled it back, Carlo gasped to see an old woman, wrapped in soiled blankets lying on a low cot. The old woman lay very still, totally and silently absorbed in her misery. She turned her face toward Pier Giorgio as he drew closer. Carlo could see now that it was covered with sores.

Pier Giorgio sat down beside her and took her thin hand in his own. The little boy, who had been staring at Pier Giorgio, now ran over to him. Pier Giorgio kissed the top of the child's head. Carlo couldn't stand it. *Watch out, Georgie!* he wanted to scream. *His head must be crawling with lice!* But the words died on his lips.

Pier Giorgio's soothing voice intoned a prayer. Then he began to talk very quietly to the woman. "Nonna, I hope you're feeling better," he said gently. "I've brought some medicine for you, and some food for everyone."

The boy's parents must be out trying to find work, Carlo thought. As he listened to Pier Giorgio's words of comfort, Carlo noticed

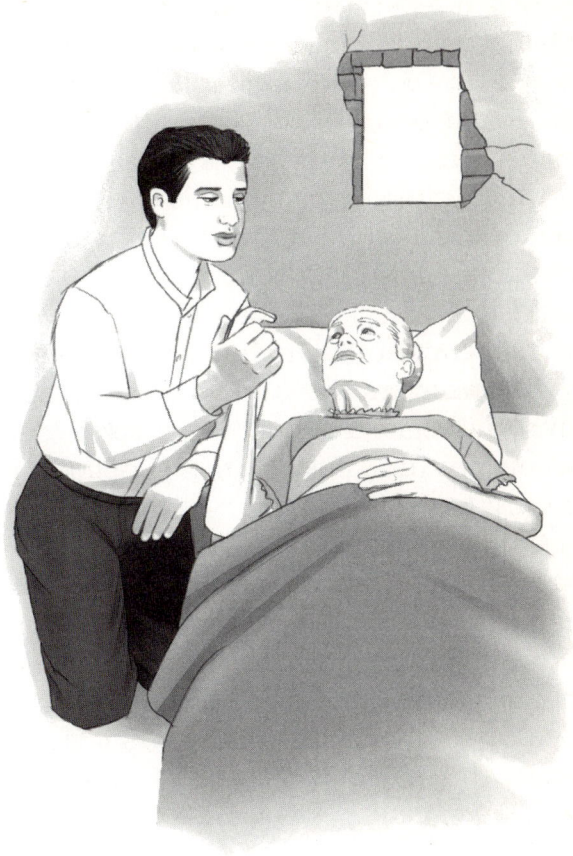

"I've brought you some food and medicine."

with growing astonishment that the entire atmosphere was changing. Pier Giorgio's compassion was literally filling the room, making it seem warmer and lighter.

The woman's face, now calm and serene, turned toward her grandchild. "I told you Pier Giorgio would not abandon us," she said weakly.

Carlo often revisited this scene in his memory. Many years later, he remembered what Pier Giorgio had told him: "Don't ever forget that when you enter the house of the poor, even a house that appears filthy and disgusting, you are getting closer to Jesus himself. He is the one who has told us, 'When you do good to the poor, you are doing it to me.'"

Carlo remarked later: "I've been working in the 'charities of Saint Vincent de Paul' for some thirty years. It was Pier Giorgio who showed me how to overcome my cold and indifferent character. Before I learned from him, I was selfish. That was it.... I was selfish."

12

A STRANGE LAND

The Frassatis experienced a special kind of excitement when Senator Frassati was appointed the Italian Ambassador to Berlin in 1920. The family moved to the German capital, leaving Pier Giorgio behind in Italy with his Aunt Elena. He would join them when he could, after finishing up his engineering studies.

Later, on his way to Berlin for an extended visit, Pier Giorgio sat on a wooden bench in the third class railroad car. He looked out at the snow-covered fields of Germany. *Will I be able to continue helping the poor?* he wondered. *What can I do in Berlin?*

Sitting across from him was an old woman. He gazed with fascination and awe at the calluses and ropey knots with which years of farm work had marked her hands. She was clutching a basket in which rested a plump white goose. "What beautiful feathers!" he found himself saying with a smile. The woman jumped in surprise and frowned. Pier Giorgio immediately realized his mistake. *I forget that I look like a foreigner,* he thought, *and, of course, she doesn't understand Italian. I'm really out of place here.*

At the Italian Embassy, Luciana welcomed her brother with a big hug.

"Don't let Mama see you in those wrinkled clothes," she laughed. "You look like someone traveling in third class."

"I *was* in third class," Pier Giorgio grinned.

"What on earth were you doing there?" Luciana asked with a hint of irritation. "Georgie, you're the son of the Italian Ambassador to Germany. You have to maintain a status. Our father's son does not travel third class."

An old argument, thought Pier Giorgio. *I don't need to travel in first class. Besides, my poor need the money I save.*

"Try to understand, Luciana..." he began, but he could see she wasn't listening.

"You'll be expected in the reception hall at eight-thirty," Luciana was saying. "And we dress for dinner. Events are more formal at the embassy." She smiled broadly. Luciana was enjoying all this.

Pier Giorgio appeared at dinner dressed in a dark suit, a crisp, white shirt and a fashionable new tie.

"Now you'll make our parents happy," Luciana whispered as she passed by. "You do look quite elegant." Actually, Pier Giorgio really did like good-looking clothes. It's just that they weren't high on his list of priorities.

After dinner, an instrumental trio was playing in the drawing room. Pier Giorgio wanted to join in the singing, but his sister pulled him over to a very tall man wearing a uniform decorated only by a small iron cross at the throat.

"Andreas, this is my brother, Pier Giorgio," Luciana said, "the one I was telling you about. He's going to be an engineer."

Andreas bowed and clicked his heels with an impressive snap. Pier Giorgio immediately noticed the faded scar that ran across his cheek. *The famous dueling scar of the German students*, he thought. The young Germans engaged in serious duels with fencing swords, and the scar was a badge of honor.

"So you're going to be a mining engineer." The scar slid up as Andreas smiled.

"Yes," said Pier Giorgio, "but I hope to do missionary work in the mines, too. The workers have such a tough time of it. In the meantime, I'm here in your beautiful city. I'm looking forward to taking in some of your famous art and wonderful music."

Andreas's face creased into a frown. "This is a beautiful city," he agreed. "In this room we see gathered such elegantly dressed ladies, and we have dined at your superb dinner table, but this is not *my* Berlin, Pier Giorgio, not *my* Germany. My Berlin is very hungry and very sad. I'd like to introduce you to it."

Pier Giorgio eagerly agreed to accompany Andreas to the "other" Berlin on the following day.

Pier Giorgio awoke early the next morning. The sun was hiding. Andreas picked him up at the embassy, and they headed for an infamous and poor district near the Alexanderplatz.

Pier Giorgio swallowed hard when he saw the throngs of refugees—Russians who had come to Berlin to escape the Communist Revolution and World War I, and Jews fleeing the massacres in which they were mercilessly killed. Crowds of men, women, and children were in rags. Many had no place to go since national boundaries had changed, leaving them without a native land, without papers, passports, or official documents to establish their identities. Some of the women carried their children like sacks of laundry across their backs. Andreas led Pier Giorgio into a boarding house. Unbathed bodies, unwashed clothing, and greasy food combined to produce a foul odor that clogged the nose. The unfortunate refugees huddled together in their despair. *Hungry, most of them are hungry,* Pier Giorgio thought.

Early in the afternoon, Pier Giorgio returned to the embassy for lunch. Afterward, he slipped away, packed up all the leftover food, and took it back to the Alexanderplatz to distribute among the refugees. Now he felt he was doing what he was supposed to be doing. That night, as he knelt by his bed with its warm goose feather quilt, he thought of how cold some of the children he had seen must be. "Please help me, dear Jesus," he prayed, "to lighten the misery of some of these people. They are so beaten and so sad."

He climbed into bed and pulled the feather quilt up to his chin. He dreamt that night of his train ride and the old woman with the goose.

A week later, Pier Giorgio, Luciana and their mother pulled up to the 200-year-old Berlin Opera House in their Rolls Royce embassy car. They had come to enjoy one of the operas of Richard Wagner, the famous 19th century German composer and a musical favorite of the Frassati family. The Berlin Pier Giorgio experienced in 1920 was a fascinating place. He loved art and thoroughly enjoyed visiting the city's many fine museums with his family. He began studying German. This would allow him to communicate with the people. It would also help him understand the plays and films he saw at the theater. The infant film industry was just getting on its feet at that time, and German movies were the finest and most exciting in the world.

But Pier Giorgio also became more and more acquainted with the "other" Germany that Andreas had introduced him to, the Germany of utter defeat, of hunger and suffering. It seemed to him that the glamorous sights and sounds he saw and heard were like a false bandage covering a huge and ugly sore.

Luciana, who loved everything about the Berlin social life, was constantly urging her brother to join her at the various balls and elegant dinners. And Pier Giorgio always made a great impression wherever he went—especially on the young women. But one night Luciana caught him in his old sports coat, his arms full of flowers.

"Georgie!" she reprimanded, "you can't go anywhere dressed like that! And where did you get those flowers? Aren't they from the drawing room? What on earth are you doing? Where are you going?"

"I'm going to a beggar's funeral," Pier Giorgio quietly replied. "I need these flowers to put on his coffin. I'll see you in the morning."

That evening Pier Giorgio walked alone behind a rough wooden coffin to the burial plot of the poor. No one else came to see the beggar off on his final journey.

No one else cared.

13

HOME AGAIN

The year 1922 found Pier Giorgio back in Turin, continuing his university studies. These were times of great danger and great change for Italy. Pier Giorgio was active in many movements, both political and religious. Because of his experiences in Berlin, he now had an even deeper understanding of the desperate plight of the poor, and he continued to visit the elderly and the sick in the Santa Chiara Hospital and in the slums of Turin.

With so many needs to fill, Pier Giorgio was always busy and usually on the run. His pockets were stuffed with notes, which he scribbled to remind himself of the day's planned errands of mercy. "Pick up the prescription for the old man with the bad cough," he read one morning. "Borrow a cart...."

Later, as he was pushing a loaded push-cart down a squalid Turin street, he heard a familiar voice call out, "Georgie, what are you doing?"

He looked back to see one of his friends from the Saint Vincent de Paul Society. "I'm helping a lady move," he said simply. "The city's thrown her out of the only apartment she could afford. I've found her another place." Since the poor woman had no one to help her, Pier Giorgio had borrowed a two-wheeled handcart from a peddler and had piled the woman's pathetic possessions onto it. He—the son of an ambassador—was her moving man.

Not long after, the Frassatis, in faraway Berlin, received a note from Aunt Elena at *Pollone*.

I felt bad that Pier Giorgio had to spend his twenty-first birthday alone with his worn-out old aunt. But he's always happy with everything. He no longer has the streetcar season ticket, but goes everywhere on his bicycle. I think it gives him a good appetite. He has to study a lot and needs to keep his strength up.

He has a friend visiting now. That should cheer him up.

Elena

As far as he was concerned, Pier Giorgio had had a great birthday. His Aunt Elena had decorated the house with his favorite flowers and made some special chocolate creams and pastries. (She knew he loved desserts.) The best part was that his good friend Camillo had come to visit.

Seated at a table with Camillo, Pier Giorgio leaned forward and opened a box of treasures, rocks he had collected on his mountain trips. "Remember where we got these?" he asked with a smile.

Camillo nodded. "On that hike we took with our friends last year, during one of your trips home from Germany."

Pier Giorgio held up a grayish, green rock. "This one's really beautiful," he admired.

Camillo looked from the rock to Pier Giorgio and replied, "Yes. It's the same shade of green as that bump on your head!"

"Keep it down," Pier Giorgio warned. "My aunt doesn't know about my involvement with the march on Rome. That fellow with the horse really got me. Out of the thousands of us protesting against them, the Fascists especially went after the Catholic students. I thought our friend from Sardinia was actually going to be run down by that cavalryman with the sword."

"He would have if you hadn't intercepted him, Georgie," Camillo exclaimed. "What a day that was!"

"The worst part is that those Fascists will have their chance to take over our country."

"Georgie, you can't change the world."

"I know, Camillo. Just don't ever mention my narrow escape to my aunt, Okay? She thinks I got this bump when I fell off my bike."

"Did you tell her that?"

"No, she just assumed it. I left it at that."

"A lot of people heard about that demonstration, Georgie."

"But no one in my family did, and I'd like to keep it that way."

"If you say so." Camillo went back to the box of rocks.

Pier Giorgio studied the green gray rock. His aunt would never understand his complicated life, especially the political activities he and the members of the Italian Students' Federation were involved in. These were getting more and more dangerous due to the emerging power of the Fascists. Aunt Elena did know that Pier Giorgio spent the last Saturday of every month in all-night Eucharistic adoration at the Church of the Consolata. She also knew that he attended daily Mass and received Communion at his parish, the Church of the Crocetta. But she wasn't aware of his personal attention to the poor and his work with the Society of Saint Vincent de Paul. She thought he simply wasted away his free time.

No one in Pier Giorgio's family understood his sometimes-desperate struggle to manage all these obligations. No one understood how hard it was to fit everything in.

Pier Giorgio's father, at times, showed more understanding toward his son. Because of his position, he knew of Pier Giorgio's dedication and bravery. He once wrote,

...I understand what your soul is all about. It's beautiful and upright, as I wished it to be. No matter what happens, don't ever change. I'm proud of you, Georgie, and I see that the few good things in my character have passed on to you. Never more than today, I send you a big hug with a faithful heart.

Pier Giorgio realized that he and his father were very much on the same page politically, but not spiritually. While Ambassador Frassati did not believe in God, he did believe in mercy and justice—especially for the downtrodden and the hopeless. This made Pier Giorgio very proud of him.

14

JOURNEY OF PRAYER

Kneeling in his bedroom, Pier Giorgio looked up at the icon of Saint Catherine of Siena. She was his spiritual mentor, a fearless woman who hadn't been afraid to tell popes, kings, and queens how to behave and who had felt equally at home with nobles and peasants. Her own parents, like Pier Giorgio's, had tried very hard to keep her from becoming a religious. She too lived in a dangerous war torn era, the 15th century. She prayed and sacrificed and eventually became a Dominican tertiary.

Pier Giorgio found himself thinking more and more of the Dominicans. He decided to seriously look into joining the tertiary Dominicans as Catherine had. "Saint Catherine," he prayed, "intercede for me. Ask the Lord to help me please him *and* my parents. Help me to serve our desperate poor."

Not even his family's attitude toward a religious vocation, however, could dim Pier Giorgio's joy. He loved serving his poor, and attending his spiritual exercises with like-minded friends. He particularly enjoyed the last Saturday of the month, when he spent the entire night in prayerful adoration at the Sanctuary of the Consolata, and his daily Mass and Holy Communion at his parish church. He never deviated from this schedule. This was his life.

The next night, Pier Giorgio went to his adoration at the Sanctuary of the Consolata, the great Baroque church in Turin and the destination of pilgrims and tourists for over 1,000 years. The Blessed Virgin has been honored under the title of Our Lady of the Consolata (Consolation) for almost 1,500 years. Pier Giorgio felt comforted by the faith of the pilgrims who surrounded him. The beautiful church with its ancient paintings and flickering candles always raised his spirit to God. He lifted his eyes to the famous icon of the Consolata. Our Lady, in a deep blue veil edged in gold, was holding the infant Jesus in her lap. *Dearest Lady*, he prayed, *help me to serve Jesus and be a good son to my parents. Let my mother understand why I come here. Help our Church in these desperate times, in her struggles with atheists, anarchists, and Communists.*

After receiving Communion at his parish the next morning, a shaft of sunlight burst

"Dearest Lady, help me to serve Jesus."

through an upper window, reaching out to him in the semi-darkness. Suddenly Pier Giorgio was back in spirit on the *Château des Dames*, a brilliant white glacier he had climbed so many times. Images of one fateful climb surged into his consciousness like so many scenes of a film. In his imagination he again felt the sun's deadly rays on his back. He saw again the dangerous signs of thaw on the glacier. He heard the tremendous rumble of the avalanche and the muffled screams of his friend Loretz as he fell and was buried by the terrifying cascade of rocks and ice. Pier Giorgio covered his face with his hands. What had been Loretz's thoughts as the rocks bore down on him in those last moments?

How fragile we are, Pier Giorgio thought. *We must always be prepared to meet the Lord, always be aware of what we have on our conscience and be sorry for the times we've offended God.*

Now, more than ever, Pier Giorgio was aware that life was fleeting. He had told friends, "The day I die will be the happiest day of my life, because I'll be lifted up to glory and see the face of God."

Loretz had already gone on to this heavenly fulfillment. Pier Giorgio had no fear of death. "That's what we're here for," people often heard him say. The ray of light had faded now, shrouding the church in shadows. Pier Giorgio continued his prayer, for Loretz, for his family, his friends, and his poor.

15

A STEP CLOSER

Pier Giorgio sat avidly reading one of his favorite books, a biography of Saint Dominic. Father Robotti, a Dominican, and his mentor at the Italian Catholic Students' Federation, had given him this volume and many of the others that filled the shelves of his study. That year, 1922, marked the 700th anniversary of the famous saint's birth. Though Pier Giorgio knew Dominic's story by heart, reading it never failed to inspire him.

Dominic (Domingo) de Guzmán, born in Spain in the Year of Our Lord 1170, began his career as a young man studying at the University of Palencia, the finest in Spain.

Even though he was one of the fortunate and privileged of his time, Dominic de Guzmán had compassion and dedicated himself to helping the poor. Books in Dominic's time were scarce and very expensive because manuscripts were written and illustrated by hand, one at a time. Nothing was done in haste. Monks copied these sacred texts lovingly and embellished them with beautiful illustrations. In spite of this,

Dominic once sold his costly schoolbooks (with all his notes in the margins) to give the money to the needy.

Dominic was a man Pier Giorgio could understand and relate to, a man who cared as passionately as he himself did about charity.

The very next day Pier Giorgio dropped in on Father Robotti.

"Father, what can I do? I'm very interested in joining the Third Order of Saint Dominic. But how will I manage it with my busy schedule? I don't want to join and then not be able to fulfill my duties."

Father Robotti folded his hands and leaned forward on his small desk. "Pier Giorgio, you know the Third Order is designed for those who live an ordinary life. The members or tertiaries don't live in monasteries or wear the religious habit of the monks and nuns. They simply wear the scapular of the Third Order, a small square of cloth on a ribbon. They live at home with their families. Some are married and some, like yourself, are single and living a regular life of work and study."

"I love what the Dominicans do, Father, caring for the poor and preaching the Gospel in different ways. I want to be a part of it."

"What you need to understand is that the rules of the Third Order have been modified in recent times to accommodate modern life," replied the priest. "Much of what you're already doing will be a part of your life as a Dominican tertiary, but you'll have the added support and companionship of those who believe in work and sacrifice as you do."

Pier Giorgio had made up his mind. "I want to join the Third Order, Father Robotti," he said with determination.

The priest smiled. "Then let's arrange for you to begin your journey."

Pier Giorgio's acceptance interview was to be in the cell of the prior of the Dominican Order in Turin. The prior was the head of the monastery, and the cell was also his living and study quarters. Pier Giorgio was guided through a wooden door into a small area with a table, a stool, and a cot. A series of shelves behind the prior's desk were lined with ancient scrolls and books. A large cross hung on the wall. Light poured in from a simple window near the ceiling.

Pier Giorgio had worn his best clothes, including the new white shirt Luciana had sent him for his birthday. Usually so confident, he suddenly felt nervous. He could feel his heart racing in expectation and excitement. The back of his neck was getting damp, and he had to resist the urge to straighten the lapels of his elegant jacket. This was his first step toward joining the lay order. This was the beginning of a life lived with people who believed as profoundly as he did, who shared his same spiritual values.

"Sit down, Pier Giorgio," the prior kindly invited.

The interview was over before he knew it. Pier Giorgio left the cell in a happy daze. He had received permission to start his training as a Dominican tertiary.

On May 28, 1922, in the San Domenico monastery church, Pier Giorgio made his first vows as a tertiary. This was a new step on his spiritual journey. He chose Jerome as the religious name by which he would be known in the Third Order. He took the name in honor of Girolamo (Jerome) Savonarola. Savonarola was a courageous Italian Dominican who had condemned the decadent Church clerics and morally corrupt leaders of 14th century Florence, suffering a horrendous martyrdom as payment for his honesty and dedication.

Jerome, like Saints Dominic and Catherine of Siena, showed bravery in the face of those more powerful than he. He remained unwaveringly committed to his Church and his faith. Because Pier Giorgio also lived in a time of political upheaval, corruption, and suffering, he greatly respected those who had endured similar chaos and evil and fought against it.

A year later, in 1923, Pier Giorgio received the scapular of the Third Order and took his final vows, becoming a full-fledged member of the Dominican Order as a tertiary. He had fulfilled one of his greatest dreams: he would now more fully serve God and neighbor with those who shared his ideals. Pier Giorgio had taken another step on his adventurous climb to the summit of union with Jesus.

16

HIGH SPIRITS

"I'm glad to see Pier Giorgio enjoying his friends," remarked Luciana as she poured Father Righini a cup of coffee. "He's really been studying too hard lately. This break is good for him. You know about that crazy group he and Marco have formed, don't you, Father?"

The priest laughed. "You mean *The Shady Characters?*"

"Yes," Luciana nodded. "They're all members of the Federation of Italian Catholic Students, but they have to be mountain climbers to belong. That's what sets them apart. I've heard that you call them *The Disaster Society*," Luciana added with a grin.

"You can't blame me, can you?" asked Father Righini, leaning back in his chair. "They do go a bit over the edge with their jokes once in a while. Like the time they sent that tiny donkey to one of their members who was slacking off in school. It's a good thing the fellow was easygoing enough to take the hint. He actually ended up improving his grades as a result of the joke." The priest set down his coffee cup and continued. "It's a fact that *The Shady Characters* have been able to create bonds of friendship and support that all the other students admire, Luciana. And your brother's high spirits and good nature are a boost to everyone in the Federation."

But the next practical joke Pier Giorgio and his friends played got them into more trouble than they had bargained for....

Members of the Federation of Italian Catholic Students were assembled in a large hall to hear a speech given by the President of the Conference of the Catholic Ladies of Turin. The leaders of the Catholic Ladies sat attentively in wooden chairs on the stage. Directly in front of them, just below the stage, *The Shady Characters* sat crammed in the orchestra pit.

Pier Giorgio's friend, Marco Beltramo, was next to him. Marco fidgeted as the president of the Catholic Ladies droned on in an impressively boring speech.

"Is she ever going to quit?" he whispered.

"Shh, be patient," Pier Giorgio replied.

Although the students were delighted when the speech finally ended, their applause wasn't very enthusiastic. *The Shady Characters* sprang into action to remedy this situation. Marco climbed onto the shoulders of Pier Giorgio and another friend so that he was high enough to see out of the orchestra pit and into the audience. He then began to cheer the students into applauding.

"For the Turin Catholic Ladies," Marco and Pier Giorgio shouted over the clapping, "a cannon shot!"

The students in the audience followed with a resounding "BOOM!" at the top of their lungs.

The hall shook with the noise. This was repeated again and again, the "BOOMS" increasing in decibels each time. Pier Giorgio, swept away by the excitement of the moment, let Marco slide off his shoulders, sending him crashing to the floor amid peals of laughter and even more shouts and whistles.

Unfortunately, the President of the Catholic Ladies did not appreciate the thunderous reaction to her speech. In fact, far from being pleased by the show of enthusiasm, she looked quite bewildered and shaken. Obviously, no one had ever shown this much gratitude for her speaking abilities.

The President of the local Federation, a fellow student named Antonio Severi, angrily jumped to his feet. When the noise began to die down, he called out, "Pier Giorgio Frassati and Marco Beltramo, leave the hall at once! Your lack of manners and bad jokes have embarrassed us all."

"We were only doing our best to make everyone feel at home and appreciated," countered Pier Giorgio. And he meant it. He had never intended to hurt anyone's feelings; he just wanted the students and their guest speakers to have a good time.

"Never mind," Severi glowered. "I told you to leave."

The next day a stern letter addressed to Pier Giorgio arrived at the local Student Federation center. It was from Antonio Severi. The letter scolded Pier Giorgio for what had happened and threatened him with all sorts of penalties on account of his "bad behavior" at the meeting. It even implied that he might, in the future, be expelled from the Federation of Italian Catholic Students.

"After all you've done for them," Marco commiserated. "Severi's forgotten your bravery in rescuing our Federation pennant from the cavalry, endangering your life in that demonstration in Rome. Ungrateful, that's what I call it."

"And what about this part here," Pier Giorgio asked with a grin, "where it says I must pass this letter on to my friend Marco Beltramo?"

"What? Let me see that!" Marco demanded. He shook the letter in his fist. "Who does Severi think he is? Just because he's the Federation president...he's only a student, like us."

Pier Giorgio laughed it off. "Severi must be the stingy type. He should have sent you a letter, too. After all, you deserve your own. He's threatening you by remote. I guess he didn't want to use two sheets of paper, never mind two stamps."

This finally got Marco laughing. And as the story spread, the other *Shady Characters* joined in the fun. Shouts of "BOOM" greeted Pier Giorgio and Marco wherever they went for the next week.

17

HOME INVASION

Pier Giorgio kept hard at work on his engineering studies. He was doing well, *really* well for him. He joined *The Shady Characters* for mountain climbs on every Sunday he could and was conscientious and faithful in the care of his poor people. He continued to attend Mass every morning, receiving the Lord in Holy Communion, and he kept up his nighttime Eucharistic adoration. It was a full schedule to juggle, but somehow he managed.

One sunny afternoon he, his mother, and a guest were seated in the living room at the Frassati town apartment, having a pleasant conversation before lunch.

"You know, Mama, I've gotten a lot out of the writings of Saint Augustine, and now I'm reading Saint Thomas Aquinas," Pier Giorgio confided.

His mother smiled. "And you were the boy whom your father criticized for being 'a little slower than most.' Well, he can eat his words. You're doing well, and you'll make a fine engineer someday, just like my father."

The servant came in to announce lunch. Mrs. Frassati, Pier Giorgio and Paola, their guest, moved to the dining room.

Mrs. Frassati glanced wistfully at the empty place at the head of the table. *Papa is missing again,* Pier Giorgio found himself thinking. *He should have come home for lunch today, if only to honor our guest.* Pier Giorgio felt an inner sadness as he thought of his parents' relationship. Mr. Frassati was so very busy with his newspaper. It was as if he paid attention to nothing else. He was never home anymore.

It was true that the Fascists had plunged Italy into one crisis after another. It was also true that Mr. Frassati and his newspaper staff were battling them in every way possible. Pier Giorgio was very proud of the brave and resolute stand his father had taken against this band of troublemakers.

"These *gnocchi* are delicious," he suddenly heard Paola say.

"They always are," he agreed. "We have the best *gnocchi* in all of Turin."

A scream shattered the peace and quiet.

"What in the world?" Mrs. Frassati dropped her spoon in her bowl with a clank.

Mariscia, the maid, screamed again. Loud crashes and bangs came from the living room.

Pier Giorgio jumped up and rushed toward the noise, shouting "Mariscia, what happened?" He nearly ran into a masked man who was trying to disconnect the telephone line in the front hall. "Drop it!" Pier Giorgio yelled, as he threw a punch, which sent the intruder sprawling to the floor. Springing to his feet, the man darted down the hall.

Pier Giorgio raced into the living room where two other burglars were smashing mirrors and lamps. One of the men was armed with a heavy wooden club.

"You're not using that here!" Pier Giorgio exclaimed as he knocked him down and wrestled the club away from him. The disarmed thief ran off, deserting his accomplices.

Out of the corner of his eye, Pier Giorgio saw the telephone line man sneaking up behind him. He whirled around in time to deliver a few blows that sent the intruder flying out of the room.

"He's got a pistol!" Mrs. Frassati screamed in terror as the assailant reappeared and reached for his pocket.

Pier Giorgio grabbed the man's arm, and finding no gun, drove him off with a set of well-placed punches.

"Where's Mariscia? Is she all right?" he gasped.

Paola ran to the balcony just as the men were speeding away in their car. "They've kidnapped Mariscia!" she shrieked. "Oh, they've kidnapped Mariscia!"

"No, no she's here, hiding under the desk," Mrs. Frassati called back, "hysterical, but safe."

After securing the front door, Pier Giorgio returned to the dining table as if nothing had happened. "Now we can finish our *gnocchi* in peace," he said.

The next day, news of the attack that terrorized the Frassati household filled the front page of *La Stampa*. Pier Giorgio's heroic actions were recorded in full.

"This will make all those holier-than-thous realize what a real hero my son is," Mrs. Frassati asserted. "He took on three of them and saved us all."

18

LAURA

The Shady Characters went wild over *La Stampa's* rendition of the home invasion and Pier Giorgio's bravery. Congratulations and notes zipped back and forth between the members and their friends. The group's secretary, Laura Hidalgo, a good friend of Pier Giorgio, worked with Marco and others to pass on the exciting news. Luciana, now in London, heard of her brother's heroics from *La Stampa's* London correspondent. Then a letter arrived from her mother, praising Pier Giorgio to the skies.

Back in Turin, things had taken a more serious turn. The Italian government had a real problem: the vandalism of the home of the popular editor of *La Stampa* was intolerable. Everyone knew it was the Fascists who had done it, upset at the Frassatis' public condemnation of Fascism. As a result of the break-in, the local police of Turin, the *carabinieri*, were sent to guard the Frassati residence. Extra police were even assigned to act as bodyguards to protect Mr. Frassati.

For eight months Alfredo Frassati spent a good part of his time trying to evade these policemen. They were a real nuisance. He didn't want anyone following him around. He wasn't hiding anything, and he felt that the police were infringing on his right to privacy. Pier Giorgio, on the other hand, took pity on the poor men sent to guard the house and his father. He used to bring them hot coffee or soup.

Meanwhile, *The Shady Characters* continued to plan outings to their favorite Alpine retreats. Laura Hidalgo was always a great help in getting things organized.

As Pier Giorgio watched many of his friends marry, he began to notice other qualities in the young women he knew. One day, when Laura was with the group, Pier Giorgio experienced a kind of revelation. *She's really a wonderful person,* he found himself thinking. He suddenly saw her as more than just a good friend. It was not only her physical beauty that attracted him, but her spiritual beauty as well. She was a brave and daring person with an open heart and a warm and loving spirit.

Pier Giorgio had met Laura in 1923, at the Little Saint Bernard, a favorite destination of *The Shady Characters*, high in the mountains. He had to admit that she was different from any of the other young women he knew. He had to admit that he loved her. The trouble now was, how to introduce Laura to his mother....

Pier Giorgio came up with the idea of inviting the young ladies who belonged to *The Shady Characters* to tea at the Frassati town apartment.

At first, all seemed to go along quite well.

"Now tell me about your parents, Miss Hidalgo," Adelaide Frassati invited. "Where are they from?"

"I'm an orphan, Mrs. Frassati," replied Laura simply.

"You have no family?" Mrs. Frassati pursued relentlessly.

"I have a little brother who is still in school. I look after him," explained Laura, unconscious of getting the third degree.

"You are a member of the Federation and..."

"And the Student's Catholic Action," Laura added with a smile.

Pier Giorgio's heart sank. His mother didn't approve of the Student's Catholic Action organization, and especially of the girls who belonged to it. She held nothing against the group's goals. It was just that the members were mostly blue collar and day laborers. This was simply not acceptable to Adelaide Ametis Frassati, a woman very conscious of her distinguished family's place in society. A young lady from the Catholic Action group would not be good enough for her son.

Mrs. Frassati's silent but clear disapproval of Laura hung heavy in the room. Pier Giorgio could not only see it, he could feel it. The invitation to tea had been a mistake.

"I really am in love with Laura," Pier Giorgio later admitted to Luciana. "She's so different from anyone else I've ever met. But I know how really upset Mama would be if I married her."

"I don't think Papa would be very pleased with the situation either," Luciana thoughtfully replied. "You know how funny he is about certain things."

Pier Giorgio nodded sadly.

Luciana took him by the shoulders. "Listen to me, big brother, you have a right to choose your own life's partner, just as I have." Luciana had fallen in love with a handsome Polish nobleman. Their wedding was planned for that January. The Frassati family, of course, approved of the young Count Gawronski.

"I know," said Pier Giorgio, "my confessor told me the very same thing. It's my right to choose whom I'll marry."

"Well, that settles that," said Luciana turning back to her desk and her wedding lists. "Now, how and when are you going to tell Mama that you love this girl whom she can't stand?"

"You know Mama's not well," answered Pier Giorgio simply.

"I've known that for years," Luciana sighed. "Our dreadful tensions at the dinner table. The constant tears. You have to live your own life in spite of it, Georgie."

"But what will happen if we leave Mama alone, if both you and I are gone? Papa is..."

"It's your life, Georgie," Luciana broke in impatiently. "You must decide."

Pier Giorgio felt hot tears in his eyes.

19

IN THE MOUNTAINS

Luciana and her fiancé, Count Jan Gawronski, were in the Frassati family living room looking at photographs. "Your brother goes very often to the mountains, doesn't he? What beautiful pictures!" the count remarked.

"No one loves the mountains like Pier Giorgio," Luciana boasted. "He goes as often as he can. His studies keep him up late every night. And when he's not in class on week-days, he's out helping the poor. He's almost finished with his class work now. He'll just have to take his exams to graduate."

"Why are the mountains so special to Pier Giorgio?"

"He feels they're an answer to the 'dangers' of city life," Luciana replied with a smile.

"Such as?"

"My brother believes that young people get in trouble when they're bored and have nothing to do. Pier Giorgio makes an effort to get his friends to go on these Sunday mountain trips as a spiritual exercise as well as a physical one. He feels this will help them become true apostles of the Lord."

"How?" asked Jan with interest.

"It will teach them discipline. You wouldn't know it just to meet him, but my brother is a great disciplinarian."

"No, I'd have never guessed it. He seems so full of life and fun, and he really does have a magnetic personality. I would never think of him as a disciplinarian."

"Well, you must get to know Pier Giorgio, Jan. He never makes it easy for himself. If the group is staying at one of the simple inns in the mountains, he'll take the coldest room. He has, through sports, taught himself to endure physical pain, fatigue, and other discomforts as a way to be ready for whatever comes. He always says we never know what we'll have to deal with in life, death and sickness in our families, serious disappointments, and failures. Pier Giorgio says self-control is very important."

❖ ❖ ❖

Pier Giorgio and *The Shady Characters* were on one of their mountain adventures, climbing up toward the Little Saint Bernard. The snow glistened in the bright sunlight.

As they reached the pass, someone called out, "Hey, can we take a break and have something to eat?" It sounded like a good idea. The climbers found places to sit on rocks and ledges in the snow. They eagerly pulled bread and fruit and thermoses of hot chocolate from their knapsacks.

"It's really great up here," Marco sighed as he and Pier Giorgio found a spot a bit further away from the others.

"How can you *not* believe in God when you look at all of this," Pier Giorgio replied biting into a piece of bread.

A few minutes passed in silence. "You're taking your time with that bread," Marco finally said between sips of hot chocolate. "Something's on your mind."

Pier Giorgio kicked some snow off his boot. "I'm worried about my family."

"About your dad? Are you going to work at *La Stampa?* You're not, are you?" Marco stopped drinking.

"No, I'm not," Pier Giorgio said slowly. "That's not my mission. I'll work as a mining engineer, as soon as I get my certificate. That should be soon, if I pass all my exams and graduate."

"Have you told your dad yet? I mean, that you're not going to work at his newspaper?"

"He hasn't asked me." Pier Giorgio seemed to be ignoring the bread he was holding.

"What? Georgie! You've got to tell him!"

"I can't tell him until he asks me," Pier Giorgio lowered his voice. "But there's more to it than that."

"Luciana's marriage. You don't like the count?" Marco's face fell.

"No, I do like him. That's not it."

"Your mother," Marco almost whispered.

"Yes, I think my father's had it with her."

"You mean..."

"I mean my mother's constantly crying. I don't know exactly why she does it. She just falls apart, now more than ever. My father is so absorbed in the national crisis, you know the Fascists taking over Italy and all that. He and his paper are fighting it. I admire him for his courage."

"Then what's the problem?"

"He's never home anymore, and when he is, he's a bear. My mother can't take it and starts to cry. She leaves the table right in the middle of dinner and goes upstairs to Aunt Elena's room. The two of them talk until she calms down. This has been going on since I was really young. But I think it's getting worse now. So does Luciana."

"That's really rough, Georgie," Marco said with concern. "What are you going to do?"

Pier Giorgio put his unfinished bread back into his knapsack. "I'll pray for my mother. You pray for her too. She has to get better."

"Yeah," said Marco, who didn't really believe this was going to happen. "Can Luciana help her?"

"No. She'll be gone in January. She's so busy getting ready for her wedding right now and..."

"And then she's going to move to Holland," Marco broke in.

"Yes," Pier Giorgio sighed.

"That could be making your mother even more unhappy."

20

THE SACRIFICE

Pier Giorgio continued his Sunday mountain climbs with *The Shady Characters* whenever he could. These were times when he could *really* relax and enjoy himself.

Meanwhile, the preparations for Luciana's wedding were going on all around him. Luxuriant and extravagant gifts arrived and were put on display in the game room.

The wedding took place in January of 1925, and the young couple excitedly left on their honeymoon.

Pier Giorgio and his family and friends watched the happy newlyweds board the train, and waved furiously as it pulled slowly out of the station. Shouts of "Goodbye!" and "Good luck!" rang through the air.

The mighty train gradually gathered speed. With each passing coach, faces in the windows blurred into nothingness. Pier Giorgio's heart seemed to stop. The train was escaping with his sister, his truest and closest friend. Tears slid down his cheeks. *She will be gone from us forever,* he thought.

The luxurious town apartment and the big estate house at *Pollone* seemed deserted and empty without Luciana. But another pain weighed heavily on Pier Giorgio. He realized he would never be able to ask Laura to marry him now. There was no one but him to take care of his troubled mother, and he had made up his mind that it was his duty to stay with her.

He wrote Luciana about his decision. She was devastated and replied,

Please, dear Georgie, please write to me again. Share all your thoughts with me. I won't be gone forever. I'll come back. I'll visit you. We'll be together again. We'll see each other. I promise. Are you happy?

Pier Giorgio sent back a note,

You asked if I'm happy. How could I not be? My faith gives me strength—and joy. Pain isn't sadness. Sadness is a sickness worse than anything else, a sickness caused by lack of belief in God. Our faith leads us—even though the way is littered with thorns. This thorny way is not the way of sadness—it's joy in spite of the pain.

Still, Pier Giorgio needed someone to talk to in person about his family problems. One afternoon he unburdened himself to Marco as they took a short hike. "My father has requested a legal separation from my mother," he said in flat voice.

Marco's face fell in astonishment. "You can't be serious, Georgie! What a disaster! What will you do?"

"I'll stay home. Be there for her," Pier Giorgio's voice cracked.

"Yeah, if he wants a divorce, it'll be a real scandal. Your dad is so well known. A lot of respectable women won't even talk to your mother if they divorce. You know how they are. Only your mom's very close friends and family will even try to understand. It'll be a problem, all right," Marco's face wrinkled with worry.

"I know," mumbled Pier Giorgio.

Alfredo Frassati was already making plans for Pier Giorgio to join him at *La Stampa*. All this praying and religious fanaticism of Pier Giorgio was total nonsense. His dream of bringing miners closer to God was not only impractical but silly, as Mr. Frassati saw it. He knew what was best for his son. He knew what was best for everyone....

"The atmosphere at my house is really sad and depressing," Pier Giorgio continued. "It's destroying my mother, Marco."

"Do you think anything can be done about it?"

"Yes. I can stay home and abandon my apostolate among the miners."

"Come on, Georgie! You've worked so hard for that. You're two minutes away from your certificate."

"But I can see what's coming..."

"What in the world has gotten into you, Georgie?" Marco asked in alarm.

"I'm beginning to see things from a different point of view."

Pier Giorgio went to his nighttime adoration that evening and prayed for guidance and strength. *I'll need them both,* he thought. *I'll need them both.*

The next day he stopped in at the offices of *La Stampa,* and headed for the desk of the chronicler, Mr. Cassone, whom he had known for a long time.

"My father has my position staked out here at the paper, right?"

"Yes," Cassone answered enthusiastically. He pointed to an adjacent workspace. "There is your chair, your desk, everything you'll need. The people in charge of your orientation have even been advised."

"I see." Pier Giorgio could barely maintain his composure. He was certainly not as calm as he was trying to appear. He could feel his heart thumping in his chest. His miners, his dreams, everything he'd worked for...gone, traded in a bargain for a desk and a chair.

But what about his family? With Luciana gone, what else could he do? His home was in ruins....

"Please tell my father that I accept the position, Signor Cassone," was all he could say.

Pier Giorgio walked out of the office and headed for the Church of the Crocetta. Falling on his knees, he prayed for the strength he would need to save his mother and his family.

21

THE HAPPIEST DAY

Luciana did come home to Turin that May of 1925, but the homecoming was a sad one. Grandmother Linda Ametis was dying.

Pier Giorgio's gracious and devout grandmother was now in her nineties and had been very sick for a long time. *She'll soon have her happiest day*, Pier Giorgio thought—*she'll soon see Jesus!*

Pier Giorgio had been studying non-stop. He was determined to complete his engineering exams despite his decision to join the staff of *La Stampa* after receiving his degree. He wanted very much to graduate, and his good friends in *The Shady Characters* were urging him on.

One day in June, Luciana passed by Pier Giorgio's study on her way to check on their grandmother. He was seated at his desk, bent over his books. Luciana couldn't help but notice how loose his clothes seemed to be.

"Pier Giorgio looks as if his jacket is way too big for him," Luciana remarked to her mother. "Is it just my imagination or is he losing weight?"

Mrs. Frassati had had a hard night. Her mother had kept her awake with her restlessness and moaning. "I know, I know," she abruptly replied. "He goes around with those baggy clothes. He looks like a scarecrow. He really needs to take more care of his appearance."

Luciana bit her lip. "Mama, how can you talk like that? You know this isn't like Pier Giorgio. He may not care much about clothes, but he always dresses neatly and looks good. Maybe something's wrong. Can't you see how hard he's studying? He's finishing up what he started, as you always taught him to."

"You're always making excuses for him..."

Luciana didn't stay to hear the rest. She was too annoyed with her mother. Look at the sacrifices Pier Giorgio had made for her. Didn't she appreciate *anything*?

At the end of the month, just a week before his final exams, Pier Giorgio and some friends went for a boat ride on the Po River. He had been looking forward to this break from his tedious hours of study. He'd also been feeling strangely weak in the last week or so, and his back had been aching a lot. He blamed this on the long hours he was spending indoors and on his lack of exercise. Late that afternoon, Pier Giorgio admitted to his friends, "I've got a terrible backache. I've never had one like this before." The pain had gotten much worse.

The next morning, he overslept. *I never do this,* he thought, perplexed. He felt so miserable that he stayed in bed. He was sick, but with what? Dr. Alvazzi, who was in the house to check on his grandmother, stopped by his room. He diagnosed Pier Giorgio as suffering from rheumatism, then hurried on.

Pier Giorgio was exhausted and could barely walk, but everyone was so busy attending to his dying grandmother that they paid no attention. That day the maid brought him some soup. He was starving and eagerly ate it, only to vomit it all up.

A family friend who had come to visit his grandmother stopped by his room later in the day and found Pier Giorgio pale and in obvious pain, leaning against the doorjamb. "Georgie, wouldn't you be better off in bed?" he asked.

"Honestly, no," he confessed. "I can't stay in bed with these awful pains."

Dr. Alvazzi came by again and gave him a sedative to help him sleep.

Later that evening, Marco came up to his room and was about to greet him with the traditional Latin hug.

"No, Marco!" protested Pier Giorgio in alarm. "I may have Malta fever, and it's very contagious."

That night, Pier Giorgio began having difficulty swallowing.

Grandmother Ametis died the next day. Pier Giorgio couldn't climb the stairs to see her. He could no longer walk.

The next morning, Friday, the family took Grandmother Ametis in a sad motorcade to *Pollone* for her burial. Aunt Elena had persuaded Pier Giorgio's mother to stay behind. "You're exhausted, Adelaide," she said, "and Georgie seems quite ill. It's better if you stay home."

When Mrs. Frassati went to check on Pier Giorgio, she found him almost totally paralyzed. She frantically called Dr. Alvazzi.

This time the doctor made a more thorough examination. His shocking diagnosis: polio.

In those days, the word was practically a death sentence. Polio was a severe infectious viral disease that inflamed the brainstem and spinal cord. It often led to paralysis and death. Victims who didn't die were severely crippled for life. No cure or vaccine for the terrible disease would be discovered until the late 1950s. Pier Giorgio had contracted the most severe form of this illness, which often attacked the young and the healthy.

When the rest of the family returned from the funeral at *Pollone* and heard the devastating news about Pier Giorgio's condition, they could barely believe it. He'd always been so strong, so healthy, so active. It seemed impossible that any illness could bring him down. Luciana desperately pleaded with the doctor to reconsider his diagnosis, but he was sure. He'd seen too many tragic cases before.

Luciana ran to her brother's bedside. His friends Marco and Camillo waited downstairs. Pier Giorgio could no longer speak. He tried to scratch out a message on a note pad with his mostly paralyzed right hand. Luciana struggled to hold back her tears as she attempted to decipher what Pier Giorgio so urgently wanted to communicate. Finally she understood. He wanted her to get medication and a pawn ticket from his coat pocket for one of his poor. He also wanted the medication delivered to this sick person. Even in his grave condition, he still thought first of others.

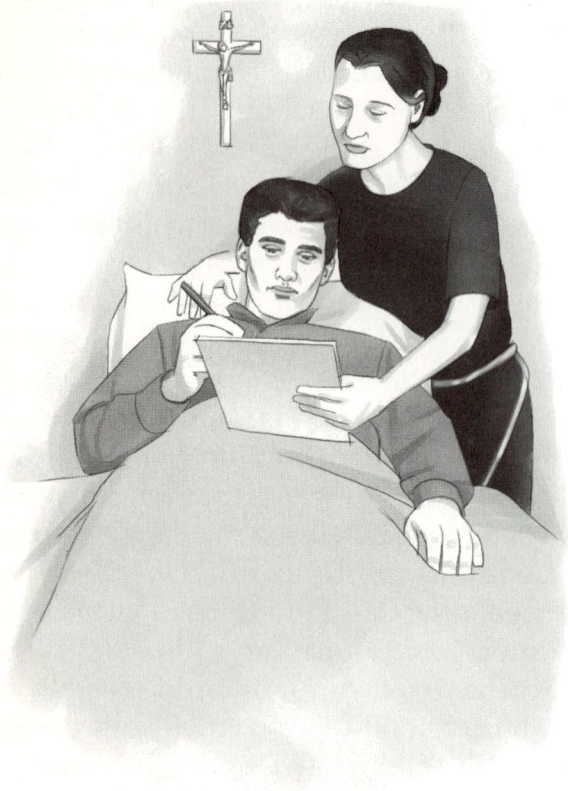

Pier Giorgio was trying desperately to scratch out a message.

Pier Giorgio's night was agony. He could barely breathe and was constantly gasping for air. One nun, a nurse, stayed with him through the night.

The next morning, the priest arrived to pray and to administer the sacrament of the Anointing of the Sick. Marco was there, watching in disbelief. Mr. and Mrs. Frassati were weeping and sobbing. Friends and family came and went, numbed by the tragedy unfolding before them. Some wept, some prayed, some were mute with sorrow.

Pier Giorgio was now completely over-whelmed by the paralysis. The once strong legs that had conquered the rocks and crags of the Alps were immobilized in an invisible vise. The voice that had sung off-key and laughed and cheered was silenced. Only Pier Giorgio's gasps could be heard above the muffled sounds of weeping and praying as the paralysis cruelly continued its work of suffocation. The arms that once carried ropes and skis were frozen into uselessness. The dark, lively eyes always filled with joy and mischief were now glazed and dull.

The long case clock downstairs tolled out the evening hour, seven o'clock. Outside Pier Giorgio's room, a mysterious gust of wind blew gently in the hall. Then all was quiet. Pier Giorgio's handsome features relaxed. The ordeal was over. He had reached the summit of his life's climb. He would now see the face of Jesus.

22

HOLINESS REVEALED

Down in the kitchen, the cook wrote on the wall calendar, "Today Saint Pier Giorgio has died." She had opened the back door to many of Pier Giorgio's needy cases. She knew how many people he had secretly helped over the years.

The news of his death spread like wildfire through Turin, from the princely palaces to the poorest slums. The Federation students carried Pier Giorgio's coffin from his room. As Luciana said, "He made the last trip down the wide staircase of our home upon the shoulders of his friends."

At nine o'clock that Sunday morning, July 6, 1925, the streets of Turin were clogged with people as Pier Giorgio's funeral procession wound its way to the Church of the Crocetta. His family was overwhelmed. "Where did all these people come from?" they asked each other in amazement. Pier Giorgio's parents, who had not understood his faith and his actions in life, began with his death to appreciate what an exceptional person their son had been and how many lives he had touched.

Numerous mourners knelt in the streets. Others reached out to touch the coffin of their beloved friend as it passed. Many sobbed and wept as they prayed. The crowd packed the piazza in front of the church beyond its capacity. These were Pier Giorgio's friends, his poor, who wished to be near him for the last time. He had had his happiest day. They believed he was now among the angels and saints.

In the months following his death, more and more people raised their voices. One would say, "Look what Pier Giorgio did for me and my family." Another would interject, "My mother would be dead if it weren't for Pier Giorgio." Yet another would tell all her friends and neighbors, "Pier Giorgio saved my little boy...." These voices proclaimed the true holiness of Pier Giorgio to all the world.

How many he had helped! *Besides* all of his other charitable activities, Pier Giorgio, at the time of his death, was financially supporting 120 poor families!

Everyone was astounded that he had done *so much* for *so many* for *so long* without ever letting others know about it. Societies were named after him. His fame grew. Everyone suddenly wanted to know more about Pier Giorgio Frassati.

After his death, his parents mended their marriage. Luciana went on to have six children of her own, all of whom she taught about their incredible Uncle Pier Giorgio, whom Pope John Paul II would later call the "Man of the Beatitudes."

On May 6, 1990, in Saint Peter's Basilica in Rome, Pope John Paul II proclaimed Pier Giorgio Frassati "Blessed" according to the rites of the Roman Catholic Church.

His beatification marked a new height for Pier Giorgio. But more importantly, it gave him to all of us as a shining example to lead us to our own summit, ever upward and closer to God.

PRAYER

Blessed Pier Giorgio, you taught me how to lead an unselfish life and to keep those who suffer close to my heart. You had good times with your friends and you really enjoyed sports. But you always kept God and love and kindness to others as your highest priorities.

Help me when I try to imitate you and I stumble. Help me when I lose my grip in trying to climb always closer to God.

I want to be an apostle of Jesus just like you. Amen.

GLOSSARY

1. **Anarchist**—a person who denies the need for any government and seeks to destroy existing ones.

2. **Apostolate**—the duties or mission of an apostle.

3. **Baroque**—highly ornamental style of European art and architecture popular from the 16th–18th centuries.

4. **Beatification**—the ceremony in which the Roman Catholic Church officially recognizes that a person has led a life of Gospel holiness in a heroic way. It is the second step toward sainthood. A person who has been beatified is called by the title *Blessed.*

5. **Communism**—a destructive doctrine of communal ownership in which everyone is equal and the government owns all. Persons who live by the principles of Communism are called **Communists**. In the 20th century, it is estimated that Communist governments have murdered more than 200 million people.

6. **Dominican tertiary**—a layperson who joins the Dominican Order and makes vows of poverty, chastity and obedience, but

remains living at home, following many of the spiritual practices of the Order and observing a special rule of life.

7. Fascists—a political organization founded by the Italian dictator Benito Mussolini in 1919. Its main beliefs were later adopted by the German dictator Adolph Hitler.

8. Fencing—the art of fighting with slender swords, considered good training in physical fitness.

9. Glacier—a large body of accumulating ice and snow that actually moves under its own weight and can be a danger for mountain climbers and skiers.

10. Gnocchi—a traditional Italian dish made from potatoes shaped like small dumplings.

11. Jesuits—officially known as the **Society of Jesus**, an order of priests and brothers founded by **Saint Ignatius of Loyola**. Its primary purpose is to educate young people.

12. Mentor—an older person who provides advice and support to and watches over the progress of a younger less experienced person.

13. Piazza—a public square.

14. Piemontese—a native of the Piedmont region in Northwestern Italy (includes Turin).

15. Sacrifice—(as used in this story) something pleasing that we give up or something difficult that we do to offer to God as a gift.

16. Sideboard—a piece of furniture with drawers or shelves used to store tableware and other items in a dining room.

17. Victor Emmanuel—King of Italy from 1900 to 1946. During Victor Emmanuel's reign, Benito Mussolini took over Italy and ruled as an absolute dictator.

18. Vow—a solemn promise made to God. Religious priests, brothers and sisters, as well as lay members of secular or third orders usually make vows of chastity, poverty and obedience.

19. World War I—a major world conflict that lasted from 1914 to 1918. Germany, Austria-Hungary, Turkey, and Bulgaria were on one side, and Great Britain, France, Russia, Belgium, Italy, Serbia, Japan and the United States on the other.

Pauline
BOOKS & MEDIA

The Daughters of St. Paul operate book and media centers at the following addresses. Visit, call or write the one nearest you today, or find us on the World Wide Web, www.pauline.org

CALIFORNIA
3908 Sepulveda Blvd, Culver City, CA 90230   310-397-8676
935 Brewster Avenue, Redwood City, CA 94063   650-369-4230
5945 Balboa Avenue, San Diego, CA 92111   858-565-9181

FLORIDA
145 S.W. 107th Avenue, Miami, FL 33174   305-559-6715

HAWAII
1143 Bishop Street, Honolulu, HI 96813   808-521-2731
Neighbor Islands call: 866-521-2731

ILLINOIS
172 North Michigan Avenue, Chicago, IL 60601   312-346-4228

LOUISIANA
4403 Veterans Memorial Blvd, Metairie, LA 70006 504-887-7631

MASSACHUSETTS
885 Providence Hwy, Dedham, MA 02026   781-326-5385

MISSOURI
9804 Watson Road, St. Louis, MO 63126   314-965-3512

NEW JERSEY
561 U.S. Route 1, Wick Plaza, Edison, NJ 08817   732-572-1200

NEW YORK
64 West 38th Street, New York, NY 10018   212-754-1110

PENNSYLVANIA
Philadelphia—relocating   215-676-9494

SOUTH CAROLINA
243 King Street, Charleston, SC 29401   843-577-0175

VIRGINIA
1025 King Street, Alexandria, VA 22314   703-549-3806

CANADA
3022 Dufferin Street, Toronto, ON M6B 3T5   416-781-9131

¡También somos su fuente para libros,
videos y música en español!